JIM BRICKMAN
VISIONS OF LOVE

Album Art © 1998 Windham Hill

Album Photography: Sandra Johnson

Additional Photography:
Courtesy of Edge Entertainment

Project Manager: Jeannette DeLisa

Art Layout: Ken Rehm

S0-DZB-889

CONTENTS

Jim Brickman, Dave Koz and Anne Cochran in the recording studio.

YOUR LOVE

Words and Music by
JIM BRICKMAN, SEAN HOSEIN
and DANE DEVILLER

8

But I could-n't ask___ for more,_____ 'cause your love is the great - est gift___ of___ all.

Chorus:

So you could give___ me wings___ to fly,____ and catch me if____ I fall.

___ Or pull the stars___ down from___ the sky,____ so I can wish on them all.

Verse 2:
In your arms, I found a strength inside me.
And in your eyes, there's a light to guide me.
I would be lost without you.
And all that my heart could ever want has come true.
(To Chorus:)

AFTER ALL THESE YEARS

Words and Music by
DAVID GROW

1. Here we are, af-ter all these years,
2. Here we are, with an-oth-er song to sing.
3. And here we are, with an-oth-er bridge to cross,

face to face, heart to heart. And I've loved you from the start, but I
All these days passed us by as we watched our child-hood fly. And I'm
face to face, heart to heart. And I've loved you from the start, but I

QUIET TIME

Composed by
JIM BRICKMAN

Moderately slow, with feeling

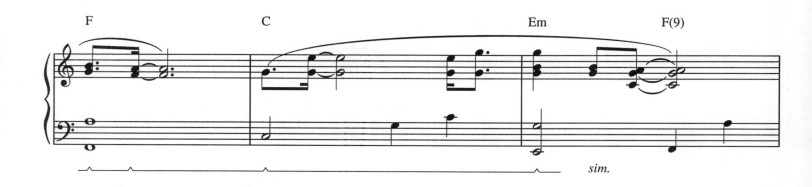

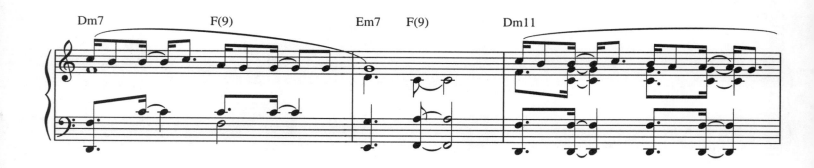

Quiet Time - 4 - 1

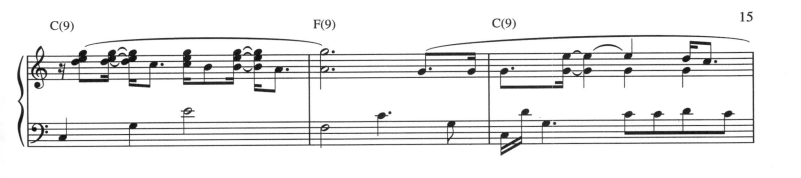

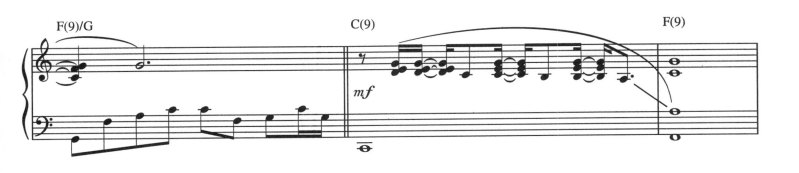

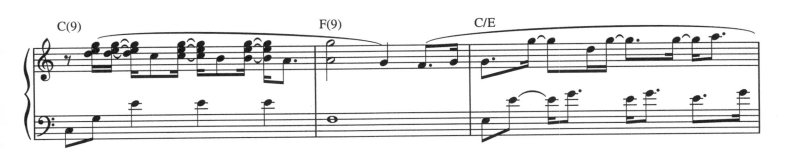

GENERATIONS

Composed by
JIM BRICKMAN

Freely, with expression

Generations - 4 - 1

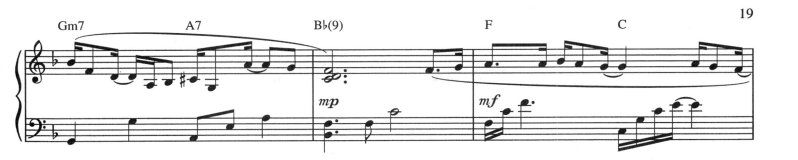

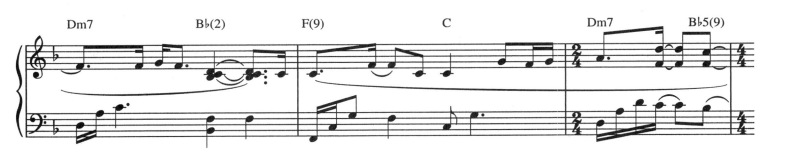

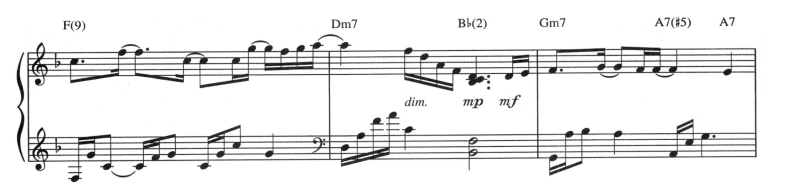

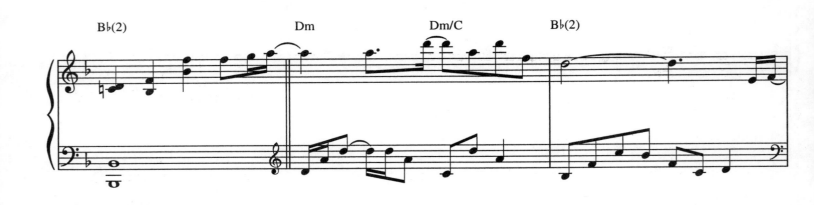

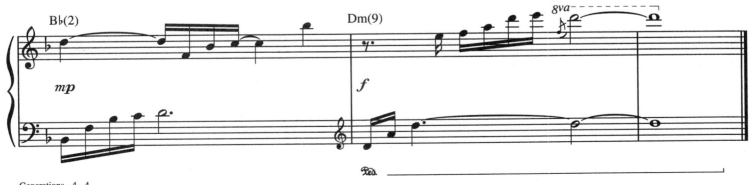

Generations - 4 - 4

WE MET TODAY

Composed by
JIM BRICKMAN

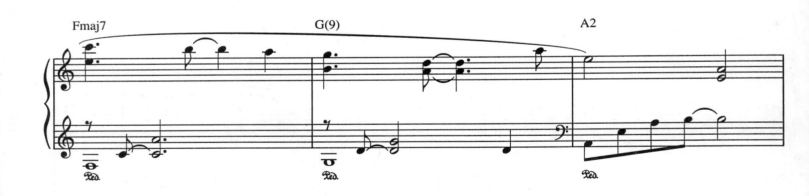

We Met Today - 7 - 1

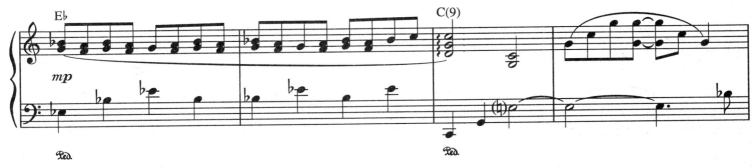

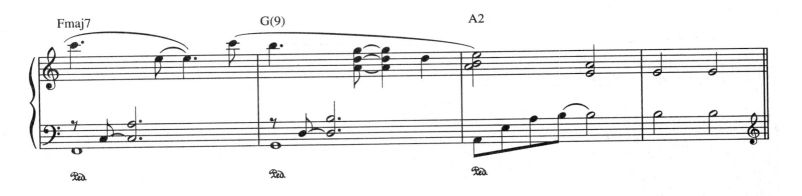

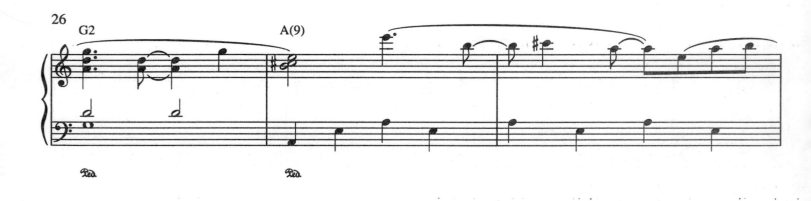

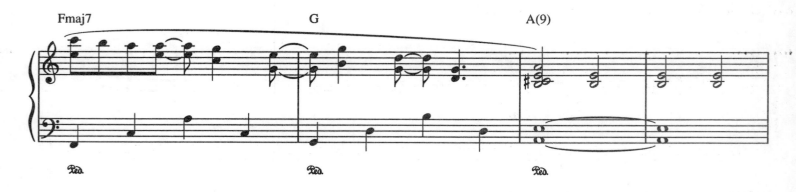

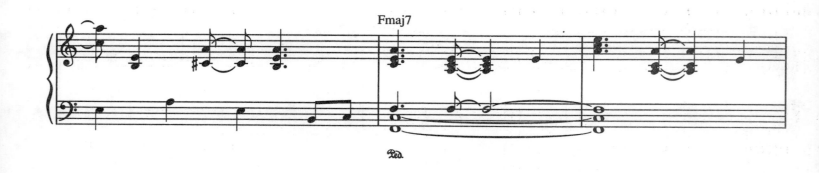

THAT'S WHAT I'M HERE FOR

Words and Music by
JIM BRICKMAN and DEAN PITCHFORD

32

PICTURE THIS

Composed by
JIM BRICKMAN

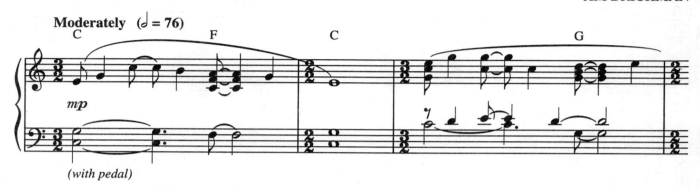

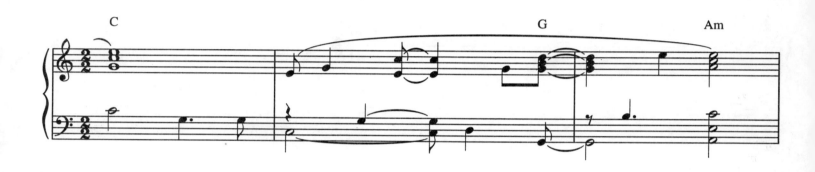

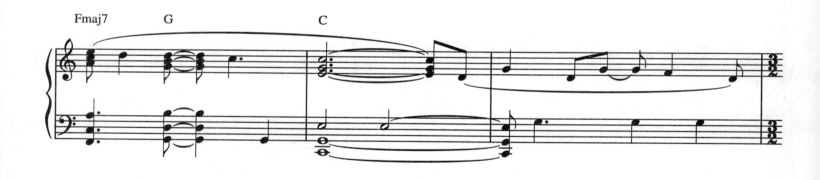

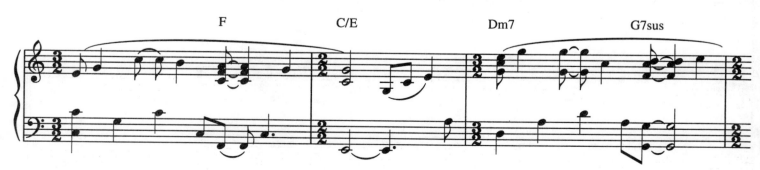

Picture This - 5 - 1

36

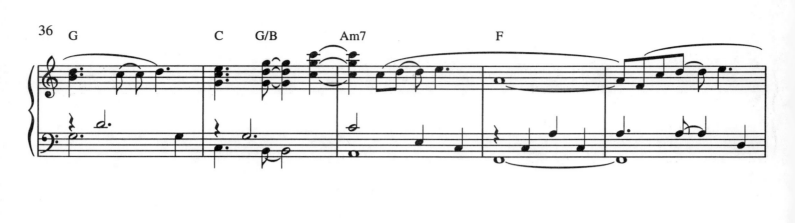

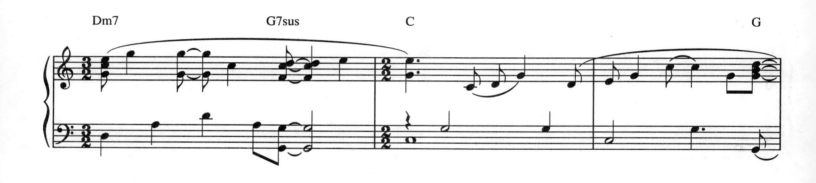

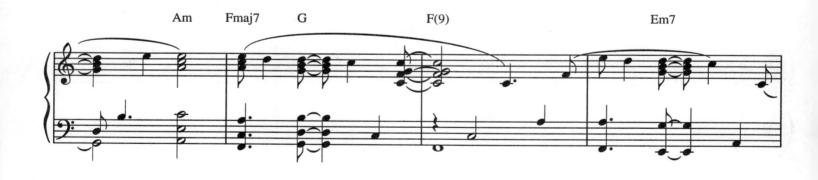

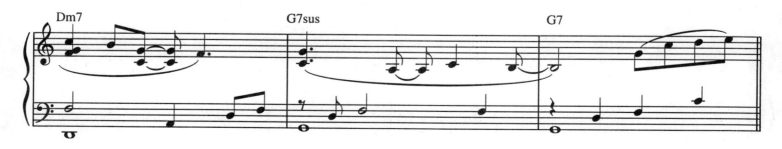

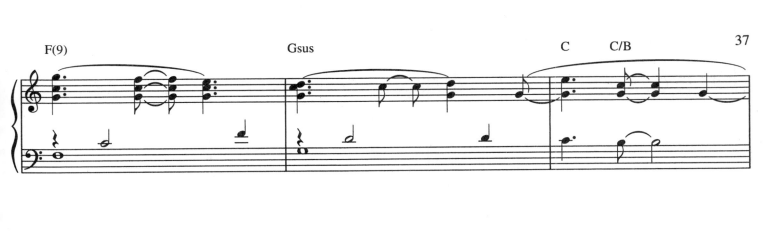

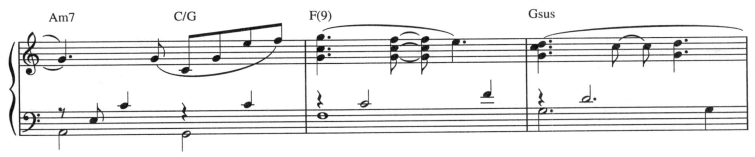

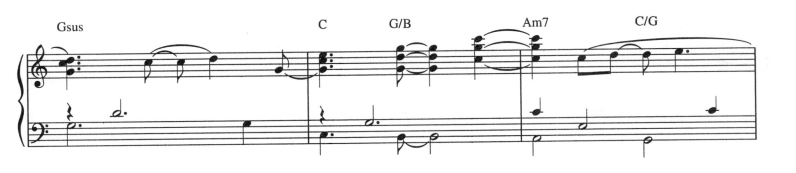

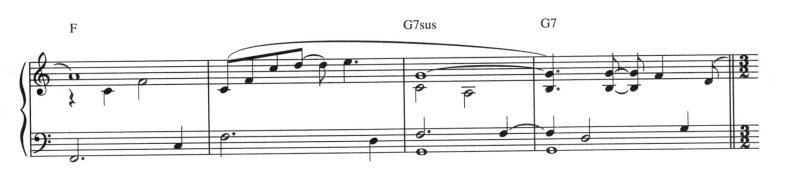

THE GIFT

Words and Music by
JIM BRICKMAN and
TOM DOUGLAS

Slowly ♩ = 72

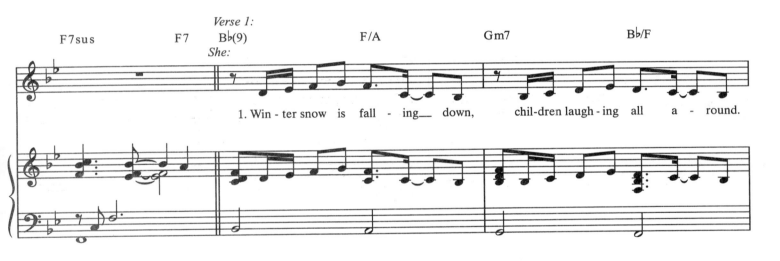

The Gift - 5 - 1

40

The Gift - 5 - 2

42

The Gift - 5 - 5

LIKE LOVE

Words and Music by
MARILYN J. HARRIS and ANGEL G. GARCIA

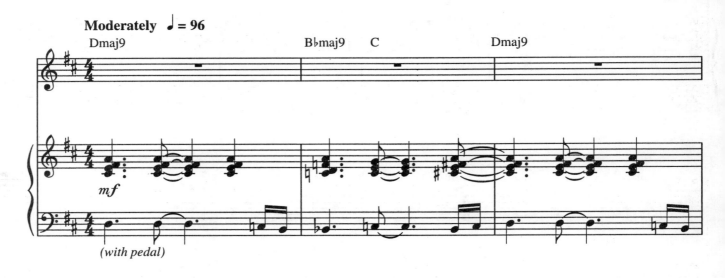

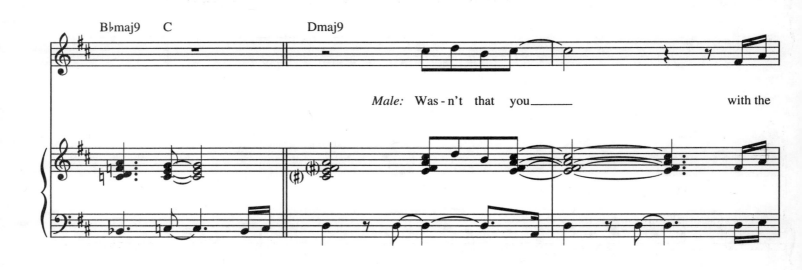

Male: Was-n't that you_____ with the

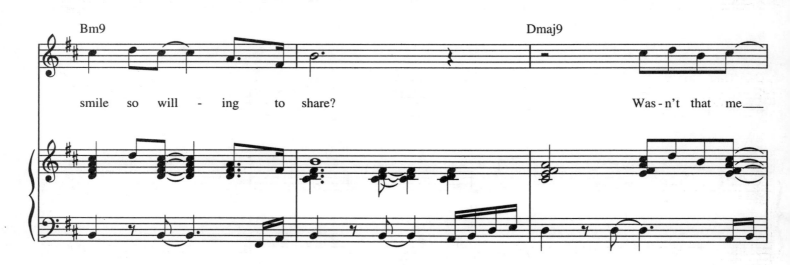

smile so will - ing to share? Was-n't that me_____

Like Love - 7 - 1

46

48

PARTNERS IN CRIME

Words and Music by
JIM BRICKMAN and DAVE KOZ

Partners in Crime - 5 - 1

52

DECEMBER MORNING

Composed by
JIM BRICKMAN

December Morning - 3 - 1

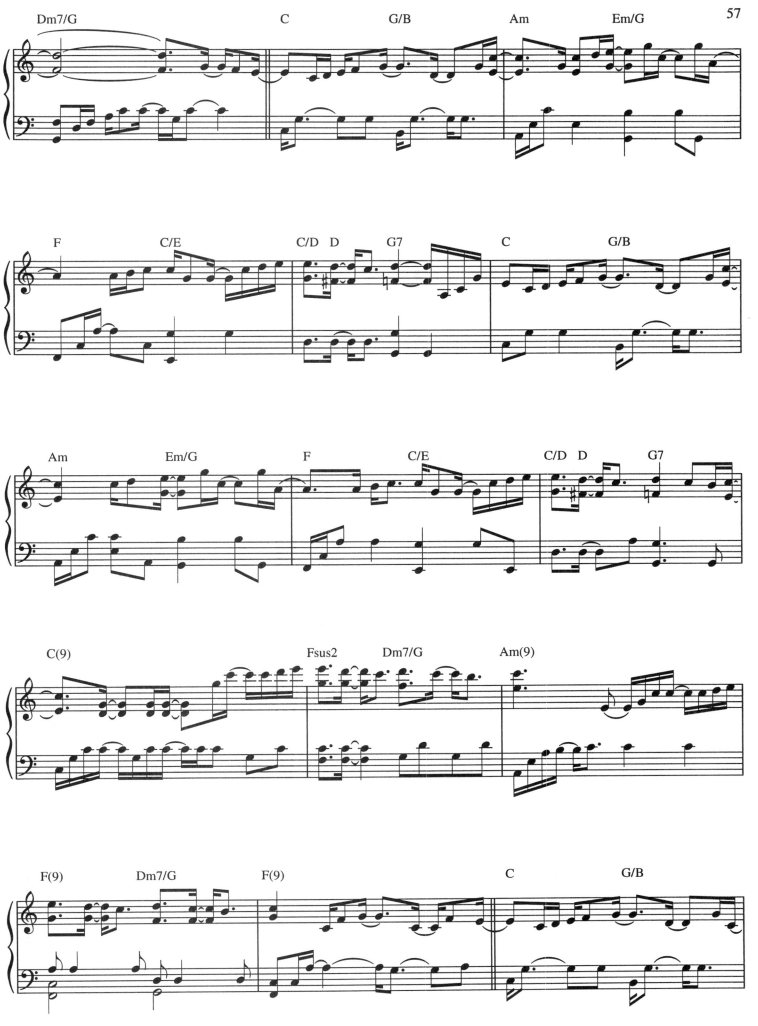

December Morning - 3 - 2

ROCK-A-BYE BABY

TRADITIONAL
Arranged by JIM BRICKMAN

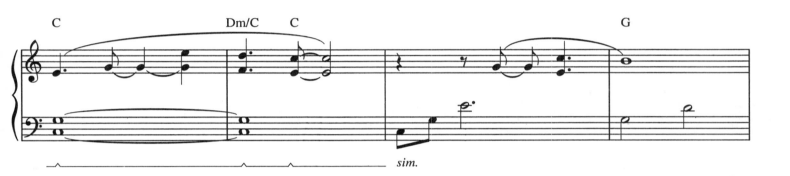

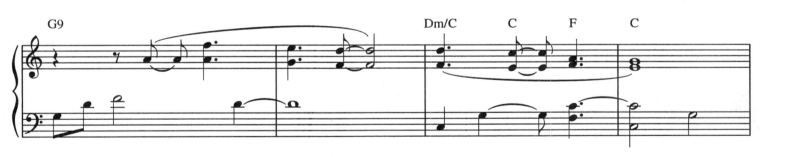

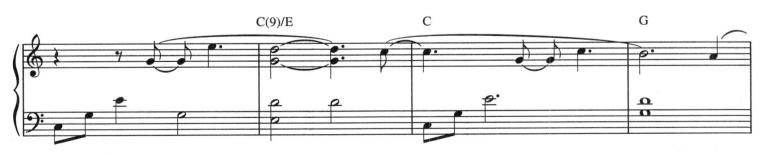

Rock-A-Bye Baby - 5 - 1

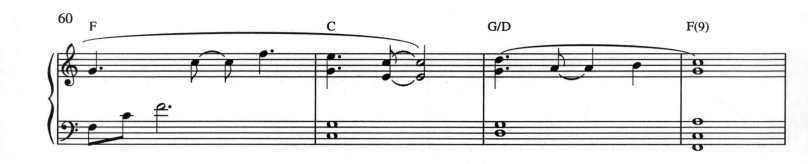

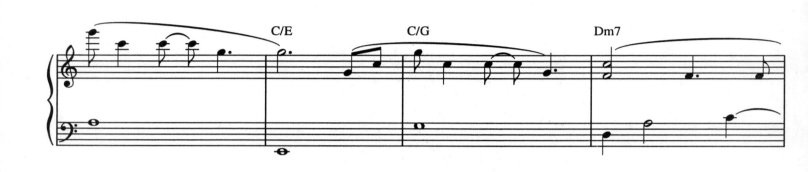

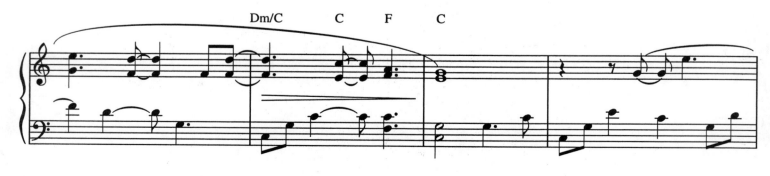

62

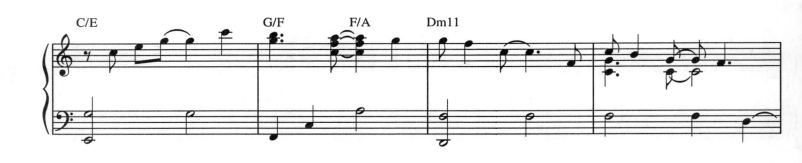

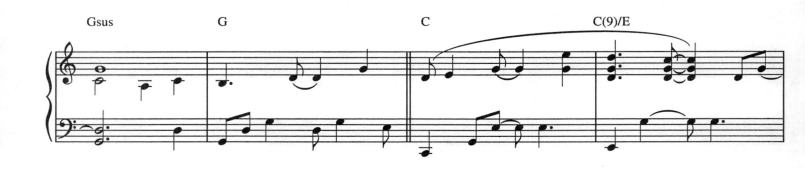

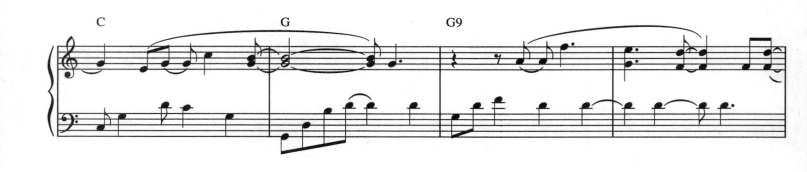

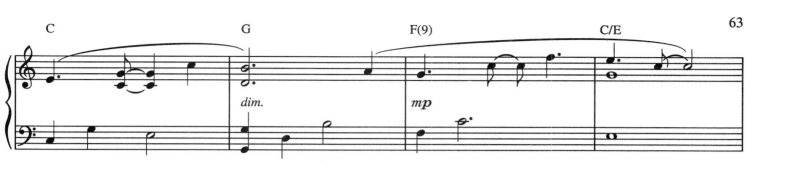

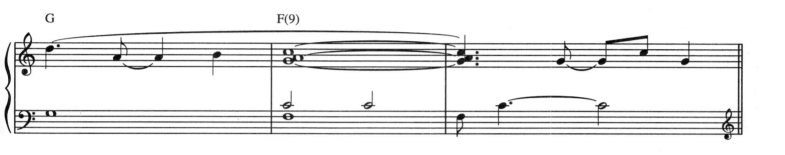

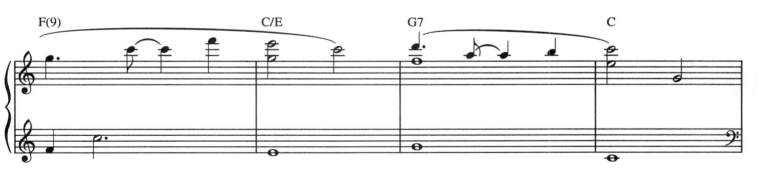

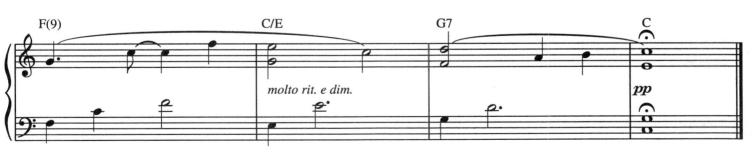

WINDHAM HILL RECORDINGS BY OR FEATURING

JIM BRICKMAN

INCLUDE:

SOLO ALBUMS:
NO WORDS
BY HEART
PICTURE THIS
THE GIFT

COMPILATIONS:
PIANO SAMPLER 2
A WINTER SOLSTICE V & VI
WINDHAM HILL SAMPLER 1996 & 1997
THE CAROLS OF CHRISTMAS
VISIONS OF LOVE

JIM BRICKMAN would like to invite you to be on his Mailing List to receive information about concert schedules, merchandise and upcoming releases. Please fill out the coupon below and mail to:

JIM BRICKMAN
c/o EDGE ENTERTAINMENT
11288 VENTURA BLVD. SUITE 606
STUDIO CITY, CA 91604

Find Jim Brickman's Web Page at **www.jimbrickman.com.**
or call **1-888-BRICKMAN** for **VIP Club Membership,**
concert tour and merchandise information.

Cut Along Here ✂

NAME _____

ADDRESS _____

CITY_____ STATE _____ ZIP_____

DOB:_____ E-Mail _____

Phone:_____

I first heard about Jim Brickman's music _____

_____

VISIONS OF LOVE